Los Angeles
SPARKS

by Luke Hanlon

Copyright © 2026 by Press Room Editions. All rights reserved. No part of this book may be used or reproduced in any manner whatsoever, including internet usage, without written permission from the copyright owner, except in the case of brief quotations embodied in critical articles and reviews.

Book design by Kate Liestman
Cover design by Kate Liestman

Photographs ©: M. Anthony Nesmith/Icon Sportswire/AP Images, cover; Meg Oliphant/Getty Images Sport/Getty Images, 4; Jordon Kelly/Icon Sportswire, 7; Ryan Sun/AP Images, 8; Alexander Hassenstein/Bongarts/Getty Images, 10; Todd Warshaw/Getty Images Sport/Getty Images, 13; Ronald Martinez/Allsport/Getty Images Sport/Getty Images, 15; Adam Pretty/Allsport/Getty Images Sport/Getty Images, 16; Lisa Blumenfeld/NBAE/Getty Images Sport/Getty Images, 19; Ric Francis/AP Images, 21; Danny Moloshok/AP Images, 23; Jonathan Moore/Getty Images Sport/Getty Images, 24; Hannah Foslien/Getty Images Sport/Getty Images, 27; Andy King/Getty Images Sport/Getty Images, 29

Press Box Books, an imprint of Press Room Editions.

ISBN
979-8-89469-015-5 (library bound)
979-8-89469-028-5 (paperback)
979-8-89469-053-7 (epub)
979-8-89469-041-4 (hosted ebook)

Library of Congress Control Number: 2025930333

Distributed by North Star Editions, Inc.
2297 Waters Drive
Mendota Heights, MN 55120
www.northstareditions.com

Printed in the United States of America
082025

ABOUT THE AUTHOR

Luke Hanlon is a sportswriter and editor based in Minneapolis. He's written dozens of nonfiction sports books for kids and spends a lot of his free time watching his favorite Minnesota sports teams.

TABLE OF CONTENTS

CHAPTER 1
RELYING ON ROOKIES   5

CHAPTER 2
LOCAL STAR   11

CHAPTER 3
BACK TO BACK   17

SUPERSTAR PROFILE
LISA LESLIE   22

CHAPTER 4
RETURN TO GLORY   25

QUICK STATS   30
GLOSSARY   31
TO LEARN MORE   32
INDEX   32

CHAPTER 1

RELYING ON ROOKIES

Rickea Jackson knew she had to make her move. With the shot clock winding down, the Los Angeles Sparks forward dribbled to her left. A Las Vegas Aces defender stuck with her. But Jackson put her head down. She drove toward the basket. Jackson then rose up for a shot. The ball

Rickea Jackson averaged 13.4 points per game during her rookie season.

bounced off the backboard and through the hoop.

    The Sparks were playing the Aces during the 2024 Women's National Basketball Association (WNBA) regular season. The Aces had won the WNBA championship the previous two years. Meanwhile, the Sparks hadn't made the playoffs in four years.

    Even so, Sparks fans felt excited entering the 2024 season. Los Angeles had two of the top four picks in that year's WNBA Draft. The Sparks used the second overall pick on forward Cameron Brink. She'd been a defensive force at Stanford University. Then the Sparks took Jackson with their next pick. She had

Cameron Brink averaged 2.3 blocks per game in the 2024 season.

been a great scorer at the University of Tennessee.

The Aces had come out firing in Los Angeles. They'd jumped out to a

Brink (22) and Jackson celebrate during a 2024 game against the Aces.

14-0 lead. But the Sparks battled back. Jackson's bank shot cut the Aces' lead to 82-80 with four minutes left. On the next possession, Brink recorded her fifth block of the game.

The Sparks soon took the lead. And with two minutes left, they led 88-86.

They ran their offense through Jackson again. She drove hard into the paint. An Aces defender fouled her. But Jackson still buried the shot. Then she made a free throw to put the Sparks up by five.

Jackson nailed a layup 23 seconds later. Her clutch scoring helped the Sparks upset the Aces. Sparks fans hoped they'd be cheering on Jackson and Brink for years to come.

GOING FOR GOLD

Cameron Brink and Rickea Jackson have each thrived playing international three-on-three basketball. Jackson played in the 3x3 Under-18 World Cup in 2019. She helped the United States win a gold medal there. In 2023, Brink won the Most Valuable Player (MVP) Award at the 3x3 Women's World Cup. She also led the United States to gold.

CHAPTER 2

LOCAL STAR

The US women's basketball team went on a world tour before the 1996 Olympics. The team wanted to build up hype for the Games in Atlanta. Center Lisa Leslie helped the team go 52–0 during the tour. Then she led the team in scoring during the Olympics. The United States easily won gold on home soil.

Lisa Leslie (9) celebrates during the women's basketball gold-medal game at the 1996 Olympics.

The popularity of that US team caught the attention of National Basketball Association (NBA) commissioner David Stern. He decided to create a professional women's basketball league. In 1997, eight teams formed the WNBA. The Los Angeles Sparks were one of those eight teams. Before the season started, the Sparks received a huge boost. The league put Leslie on the Sparks' roster. Leslie had grown up

WE GOT NEXT

The WNBA promoted its stars before its first season. Lisa Leslie, Rebecca Lobo, and Sheryl Swoopes were the main focus. Those players had all won gold in Atlanta. The WNBA aired a commercial with those stars in 1997. It featured the three players walking into an arena. At the end of the ad, the screen displayed the WNBA's slogan: "We Got Next."

Leslie (9) shoots over Rebecca Lobo during the first-ever WNBA game.

in Compton, California. She'd also played college ball at the University of Southern California. Now she would be playing professionally in her home state.

On June 21, 1997, the Sparks took part in the first WNBA game. They faced the

New York Liberty. The game featured two of the league's biggest stars. Leslie had played with New York's Rebecca Lobo at the 1996 Olympics. A crowd of more than 14,000 fans watched the two stars battle. They saw the Liberty defeat the Sparks 67–57.

Leslie shined in the WNBA right away. She used her 6-foot-5 (196-cm) frame to rack up points and rebounds. But the Sparks struggled to win games. Leslie led the Sparks to the playoffs for the first time in 1999. However, the Houston Comets swept Los Angeles in the semifinals.

The Sparks came back stronger in 2000. They lost only four games during

Two Sparks players pressure Houston's Sheryl Swoopes during a 2000 game.

the regular season. Once again, they faced the Comets in the semifinals. The Comets swept the series on their way to a fourth straight WNBA title.

CHAPTER 3

BACK TO BACK

The Sparks bounced back in 2001. Lisa Leslie had her best season yet. She won the WNBA MVP Award. Los Angeles entered the playoffs with the league's best record. The Sparks faced the Comets in the first round. Leslie wouldn't let the Sparks lose to Houston again. She recorded 47 points

Leslie (9) averaged 19.5 points and 9.6 rebounds per game in the 2001 season.

and 29 rebounds in two games to help the Sparks sweep the Comets.

Ending Houston's run gave the Sparks a boost. They made it all the way to the WNBA Finals. The Charlotte Sting were no match for Los Angeles. Leslie lifted the Sparks to their first championship.

The Sparks continued to roll in 2002. So did Leslie. On July 30, the Sparks faced the Miami Sol. During the first quarter, Leslie stormed down the court on a fast break. With no defenders around her, she dunked the ball. Leslie became the first player to dunk in a WNBA game.

The Sparks won their first four games in the 2002 playoffs. They then met the Liberty in the WNBA Finals. Los Angeles

Leslie dunks in a WNBA game for the first time.

swept New York to finish off an undefeated playoff run. Leslie won the Finals MVP Award for the second time.

The Sparks had become the WNBA's team to beat. Los Angeles made a run back to the WNBA Finals in 2003. The Sparks won Game 1 of the series. But the Detroit Shock battled back. They won the next two games to secure the championship.

Leslie kept the Sparks competitive for years. However, she missed the 2007 season to have a baby. Without their star, the Sparks struggled. They finished the season with the league's worst record. The bad season soon turned into a positive, though.

LOS ANGELES LEGEND

Michael Cooper played with the Los Angeles Lakers for 12 seasons. He helped them win five NBA titles. Cooper took over as the Sparks' head coach in 2000. He led the team to two championships in three Finals appearances.

The Sparks celebrate after winning the 2002 WNBA title.

The Sparks received the top pick in the 2008 draft. They used the pick on Candace Parker. She would soon help the Sparks return to their winning ways.

SUPERSTAR PROFILE

LISA LESLIE

When Lisa Leslie was in middle school, she stood 6 feet (183 cm) tall. She didn't play basketball at the time. But in seventh grade, a friend convinced her to try the sport. Once she played, Leslie couldn't get enough.

Leslie's height allowed her to control games in the paint. She could score over smaller defenders. And she could block shots with ease. Leslie had more than just height, though. From a young age, she learned to dribble with either hand. She could also use either hand to score near the basket.

Leslie's skills helped her win three WNBA MVP Awards. The league also named her the Defensive Player of the Year twice. Leslie helped her team win, too. She lifted the Sparks to two WNBA titles. And she won four Olympic gold medals with the US women's basketball team.

Leslie (9) averaged 2.3 blocks per game in her WNBA career.

CHAPTER 4

RETURN TO GLORY

Candace Parker took the league by storm. She won the MVP Award as a rookie. Similar to Lisa Leslie, Parker had both size and skills. The duo led Los Angeles to the semifinals in 2008 and 2009.

Leslie retired after the 2009 season. Parker continued to play well without her mentor. But the team suffered

Candace Parker averaged 18.5 points per game during her rookie year.

two straight losing seasons. The Sparks then got the top pick in the 2012 draft. Los Angeles selected forward Nneka Ogwumike. She quickly helped turn the team around. Making the playoffs became a routine for Los Angeles.

Everything came together for the Sparks in 2016. Ogwumike won the MVP Award. And she helped Los Angeles reach the Finals. The Minnesota Lynx were waiting for them. The Lynx were the defending champs. They were also the only team ahead of the Sparks in the 2016 standings.

The series came down to a decisive Game 5 in Minnesota. Down 76–75 with six seconds left, the Sparks missed a

Nneka Ogwumike takes the game-winning shot in Game 5 of the 2016 Finals.

shot. Ogwumike grabbed an offensive rebound, though. Then she scored to put Los Angeles ahead with three seconds left. Her clutch basket secured the title for the Sparks.

Parker and Ogwumike helped the Sparks return to the Finals in 2017. In Game 1, guard Chelsea Gray hit a jump shot with two seconds left. That bucket lifted the Sparks to an 85–84 win. Again, the series went to a Game 5. But this time, the Lynx won the title.

The Sparks remained a contender for the next few years. However, Parker left the team after the 2020 season. In 2021, the team missed

STEADY IMPROVEMENT

The Sparks traded for Chelsea Gray during the 2016 draft. Gray came off the bench throughout the 2016 season. But she proved to be a key part of the team's championship run. By 2017, Gray became a regular starter. She went on to make the All-Star Game three times with Los Angeles.

Two Lynx defenders contest Chelsea Gray's game-winning shot in Game 1 of the 2017 Finals.

the playoffs for the first time in 10 years. After the 2023 season, Ogwumike left the team as well. Suddenly, the Sparks' championship core was gone. The team drafted Cameron Brink and Rickea Jackson in 2024. Fans hoped they would become the next championship duo in Los Angeles.

QUICK STATS

LOS ANGELES SPARKS

Founded: 1997

Championships: 3 (2001, 2002, 2016)

Key coaches:
- Michael Cooper (2000-04, 2007-09): 167-85, 25-13 playoffs, 2 WNBA titles
- Carol Ross (2012-14): 58-32, 3-4 playoffs
- Brian Agler (2015-18): 85-51, 13-9 playoffs, 1 WNBA title

Most career points: Lisa Leslie (6,263)

Most career assists: Candace Parker (1,331)

Most career rebounds: Lisa Leslie (3,307)

Most career steals: Nneka Ogwumike (549)

Most career blocks: Lisa Leslie (822)

Stats are accurate through the 2024 season.

GLOSSARY

clutch
Having to do with a difficult situation when the outcome of the game is in question.

commissioner
The person who runs a sports league.

draft
An event that allows teams to choose new players coming into the league.

fast break
A play in which a team moves the ball up the floor quickly.

paint
The area between the basket and the free-throw line.

professional
Paid to do something as a job.

rookie
A first-year player.

swept
Won all the games in a series.

upset
To earn an unexpected victory against a supposedly stronger team.

TO LEARN MORE

Hanlon, Luke. *Lisa Leslie: Basketball Legend*. Press Box Books, 2024.
Mahoney, Brian. *GOATs of Basketball*. Abdo Publishing, 2022.
O'Neal, Ciara. *The WNBA Finals*. Apex Editions, 2023.

MORE INFORMATION

To learn more about the Los Angeles Sparks, go to **pressboxbooks.com/AllAccess**. These links are routinely monitored and updated to provide the most current information available.

INDEX

Brink, Cameron, 6, 8–9, 29

Charlotte Sting, 18
Cooper, Michael, 20

Detroit Shock, 20

Gray, Chelsea, 28

Houston Comets, 14–15, 17–18

Jackson, Rickea, 5–6, 8–9, 29

Las Vegas Aces, 5–9
Leslie, Lisa, 11–14, 17–20, 22, 25
Lobo, Rebecca, 12, 14

Miami Sol, 18
Minnesota Lynx, 26, 28

New York Liberty, 14, 18–19

Ogwumike, Nneka, 26–29

Parker, Candace, 21, 25, 28

Stern, David, 12
Swoopes, Sheryl, 12